"This is a very powerful book on the most important subject in the Bible. Yet, few Christians in the West understand the blood covenant. I hope many will read it."

—Richard Booker

Teacher and author of *The Miracles of the Scarlet Thread* as well as numerous other books

"It is refreshing to read a book when you know that the author not only talks the talk but also walks the walk. Peggy Park has written with conviction that the blood of Jesus forgives, cleanes, and heals. She very effectively communicates these truths from God's Word and from having applied them in her own life experiences."

—James M. McGee

Retired Minister of Education/Evangelism
Porter Memorial Baptist Church
Lexington, Ketucky
Presently serving as a Church Planter
and Church Development Strategist

"Unparalleled. Beyond must-read. Every believer should want to read this! There has never before been such an in-depth study of the Blood of the Lamb . . . a previously untapped, underestimated topic. With style and keen attention to detail, Peggy Park has skillfully unveiled both the intricacies and the enormity of the power of the Blood of Jesus, and in so doing has created one of the most compelling, need-to-know guidebooks ever written on this topic. A triumph!"

—Dudley C. Rutherford

Senior Pastor Shepherd of the Hills Church
Porter Ranch, California

The Power OF THE LAMB'S BLOOD

PEGGY PARK

WINEPRESS WP PUBLISHING

Packaged by WinePress Publishing, PO Box 428, Enumclaw, WA 98022. The views expressed or implied in this work do not necessarily reflect those of WinePress Publishing. The author is ultimately responsible for the design, content and editorial accuracy of this work.

ISBN 1-57921-728-1
Library of Congress Catalog Card Number: 2003114195

Dedication

This book is dedicated to the Holy Spirit, my teacher to God, my Abba Father and to Jesus, my Elder Brother, High Priest, and my Savior. May the Godhead be praised and glorified through the knowledge imparted in this book.

Table of Contents

Preface

The Power of the Lamb's Blood was birthed over several years of study on the mystery of His divine blood. The seed of inspiration to write this book was planted when an invitation came to speak before a group of believers on the subject of the blood.

I had wanted to decline, because my knowledge of the blood was so limited. I suggested I speak on a subject of which I had better understanding. The challenge came again to speak on the blood. I relented, and preparation for the presentation was the beginning of my journey of discovery into the depths of the divine blood provisions.

Yes, I was a believer but I had never been taught about the blood covenant entered into at the time of my salvation. The divine blood is the cord that binds believers together in the family of God.

Through Jesus Christ our Lord, we are bound to God the Father, whose divine blood flowed through our Savior unto all who would receive the provision of the blood for remission of sins and entrance into the kingdom of God. The believer has been redeemed, cleansed, justified, and sanctified. He has access to the Holy of Holies and the privilege of living with a clear conscience.

Acknowledgments

I am thankful to God for my wonderful husband, George, who is a great source of strength and help to me in my writing endeavors, as well as in my entire life.

I am also indebted to Myra Strand who started me on the journey of studying the blood.

My good friend Kathy Mitchell has blessed me with her secretarial skills. Donna Farmer graciously used her English background to polish my grammar and made many helpful suggestions as this book was being planned. I am grateful to my sister in the Lord, Brenda Kovacic, who did the final editing. Sue Dodd made time in her busy schedule to fine tune the book proposal.

The bill fold blood card was inspired and designed by Jessica Kidwell.

Introductory Statement

*T*here is no greater mystery in the Christian faith than the blood of our Lord and Savior Jesus Christ. Believers are challenged not to limit the power of His holy blood to the natural mind's understanding. It is my prayer that you will be greatly blessed with a deeper grasp of the benefits the shed blood of Jesus Christ made available to His followers. I also pray that you will be blessed in revelation knowledge into the vastness and incomprehensible depths of the provisions of the shed blood of the Holy Lamb of God and encouraged to proclaim the power of His blood over situations in your life and the lives of others God brings to you for ministry.

"And according to the law almost all things are purified with blood, and without shedding of blood there is no *remission*."

(Hebrews 9:22 NKJV)

"But your iniquities have separated you from your God;
And your sins have hidden His face from you."

(Isaiah 59:2 NKJV)

Chapter 1

· ·

The Necessity of a Blood Sacrifice: The Meaning of a Blood Covenant

ges ago God created the first man and woman, Adam and Eve, and placed them in the magnificent Garden of Eden. Genesis 3:8–11 tells us God came and walked in the garden and talked to His creation. What a beautiful picture of fellowship between God and His human creations!

The Fall of Adam

Adam and Eve were formed with a free will and they chose to exercise their free will in breaking the one restriction God had laid down. Their heavenly Father had told them they could freely eat of any tree in the garden except the tree of the knowledge of good and evil. That tree was declared off limits! God cautioned them that should they eat of it they would surely die (Genesis 3:3).

Satan came to Eve in the form of a serpent and said, *"Did God really say 'You must not eat from any tree in the garden?'"* (Genesis 3:1b NIV). *"'You will not surely die,' the serpent said to the woman, 'For God knows that when you eat of it your eyes will be opened, and you will be like God, knowing good and evil'"* (Genesis 3:4,5 NIV). Eve chose to listen to Satan as he placed doubt in her mind about her Lord.

She ate of the forbidden fruit. Adam in turn was snared by the lie and disobeyed God, thus breaking fellowship with Him. Sin had entered the paradise.

Adam and Eve Uncovered

Adam and Eve's innocence was lifted! They knew they were uncovered—naked before a Holy God. They had eaten of the tree of the knowledge of good and evil, and their sin and physical bodies were naked before an omnipotent, omniscient, all-seeing God. Consequently, Father God took the skins of animals and made clothes for his children. It is consistent with the Old Testament picture of blood sacrifices as atonement for sins to assume God sacrificed animals from the garden rather than directly creating skins. If this is a correct assumption, blood was involved in providing a covering for Adam and Eve.

The life of flesh was taken to provide the blood covering for their disobedience. The skins of the animals covered them physically. The blood provided a covering for their sins. This was the first foreshadowing of the necessity of blood in regard to man's sin.

Centuries later, Jesus' death provided the blood which make possible man's atonement, which is the state of being reconciled to God the father. The blood provides the payment for one's offenses if a person chooses to receive the sacrifice made for him. Under the Old Covenant sins were *covered* by blood. Under the New Covenant they are *removed*.

Through the centuries, man has continued to be confronted by Satan's words, *"Has God indeed said?"* (Genesis 3:1b NKJV). Adam and Eve yielded to Satan's suggestion, and in their disobedience an inroad was opened that set up doubt in the word of Father God.

Since Adam's fall, doubt has continued to plague mankind down through the ages. The full account of the fall of man is recorded in Genesis 2:15–17 and 3:1–6.

The Holiness of God

God is a holy God and cannot look upon sin. The word spoken through Isaiah the prophet tells us *"But your iniquities have separated you from your God; and your sins have hidden His face from you"* (Isaiah 59:2 NKJV). Hebrews 9:22 NKJV teaches, *"And according to the law almost all things are purified with blood, and without shedding of blood there is no remission."* Scripture does not specifically tell us why God chose blood to cover sin. Yet, Scripture is replete with examples of the power in the blood.

Leviticus, the book of the priesthood, tells us that blood represents life. Clearly the life of the flesh, the physical body is in the blood. *"For the life of the flesh is in the blood and I have given it to you upon the altar to make atonement for your souls, for it is the **blood**, that makes atonement for the soul"*

(Leviticus 17:11 NKJV). Blood sacrifices to cover sin were a regular part of the Israelites' life in the Old Testament. The Aaronic priesthood was responsible for carrying out the sacrifices on a day-to-day basis with the high priest responsible for the yearly atonement at Yom Kippur. This was the day the Levitical priest entered the Holy of Holies which was the innermost part of the tabernacle behind the veil. Only the high priest could enter. He offered a blood sacrifice for the sins the Children of Israel had committed throughout the year. The sins were not removed, but were merely rolled forward to the next year. The New Testament believer's sins are removed through the atoning work of the perfect lamb Jesus Christ as He shed His holy blood at Calvary.

Jesus' Blood Sacrifice

The physical covering of Adam and Eve with the bloody skins of slain animals was an Old Testament picture of the New Testament covering provided by Jesus, the last Adam. His blood made provision for the body, soul, and spirit of the new covenant man. The first Adam forfeited his unhindered fellowship with his Creator.

Jesus, The Last Adam

The last Adam (Jesus) provided a way for sinful man to come back into fellowship with a Holy God. "*So it is written: "The first man Adam became a living being, the last Adam, a life giving spirit. The spiritual did not come first, but the natural, and after that the spiritual. The first man was of the dust of the earth, the second man from heaven. As was the earthly man, so are those who are of the earth; and as is the man from heaven, so also are those of heaven. And just as we have borne the like-ness of the earthly man, so shall we bear the likeness of the man from heaven"* (1 Corinthians 15:45–49 NIV).

Lamb of God

Chapter 1:29, 36 (NKJV) in the Gospel of John both refer to the Lamb of God who takes away the sin of the world. In each reference John said, *"Behold the Lamb of God who takes away the sin of the world."* We know God foreknew from the creation of the world that Jesus would die for the sins of mankind (Revelation 13:8). Scripture clearly shows blood sacrifices as the means of atonement for sin throughout the Old Testament. In the New Testament, Jesus fulfilled the blood requirement. *"So Christ was offered once to bear the sins of many"* (Hebrews 9:28a NKJV). He became the blood sacrifice to cover the sins of any man, woman, or child who would receive that covering. We enter into a blood covenant when we receive Him into our lives as Savior. We are marked with His blood when we accept His sacrifice to remove our sins.

Under the Old Testament covenant the sin nature was still in man. The sin was only *covered* by the sin offerings made by the priests. In the New Testament, under the New Covenant, provision is made for our sins to be *removed*. The Scriptures confirming this truth are listed later in Chapter Six of this book.

The Hebrew word covenant means "to cut." In many primitive countries today the concept of blood covenant is still practiced. At the time of the entering into a primitive blood covenant, the two people involved come forward or have a representative do so. Friends, along with a priest, are present. Wine is brought forward and gifts are exchanged. An incision is made in the arm of each of the two parties and blood is dripped into the wine. The wine and blood are mixed and both parties drink from the cup. Often their wrists are held together until their blood is mingled. They are now blood brothers. What belongs to one belongs to the other. They have entered into a sacred vow. This covenant will be honored to the third and fourth generations. I am grateful to E.W. Kenyon's book, *The Blood Covenant,* for this concept and also the following account of Henry Stanley's experience in Africa.

In the 1870s, the noted journalist Stanley searched throughout Central Africa for the lost missionary, David Livingston. Stanley encountered a powerful tribe and experienced many difficulties during that search. On one occasion it was suggested to him that he cut a covenant with the chief who coveted Stanley's goat. This "letting of blood" involved a sacrifice on Stanley's part as he was in ill health and subsisted on the milk of his goat. However, Stanley's consent to the covenant practice proved to be a blessing.

In exchange for the goat the chief gave Stanley his seven-foot copper spear. The chief's spear was recognized throughout Africa, and Stanley found the natives honoring and submitting to him because he possessed the spear, which represented the powerful chieftain.

After Stanley and the chief's covenant ceremony was completed, the chief declared Stanley to be his blood brother. Blessings were pronounced. Curses were declared if the covenant should ever be broken. Scripture does not endorse this pagan ritual, but an account of it does demonstrate the place of blood in the making of covenants from ancient times to the present.

The Neccessity of a Blood Sacrifice:
The Meaning of a Blood Covenant

We recall that when Adam and Eve's innocence was lifted they knew they were naked. God's clothing of Adam and Eve, involving animal blood, was a sign of the redemption and deliverance that was to come through the blood sacrifice of Jesus Christ—the Lamb of God.

"For by one offering He has perfected forever those who are being sanctified" (Hebrews 10:14 NKJV). *"For God so loved the world that He gave His only begotten Son, that whoever believes in Him should not perish but have everlasting life"* (John 3:16 NKJV). Those who receive this gift of salvation make up Christ's church. His church is the universal body of believers that cuts across denominational and racial lines. We are astounded to read in Acts 20:28 that God purchased the church with *His own blood*. This is a great mystery beyond the full comprehension of man.

Unworthy of the Blood

Jeff Ross © 1982 Word Music, LLC

I know not why a sovereign King
Would leave His home on high
To dwell here in this barren land
With mortals such as I
He left his home in paradise
O why I'll never know
But His precious blood has made me purer
Than the virgin snow.

Here I am unworthy of the blood
Unworthy of the blood that set me free

Here I am so unworthy of the blood
Yet it flowed for me

Every time I falter
And bring the Father shame
A drop of His precious blood
Falls upon my name
I'll never know the reason why
This thing has come to me
All I know is that He did it
All for you and me
Here I am so unworthy of the blood
Unworthy of the blood that set me free
Here I am so unworthy of the blood
Yet it flowed for me

PRAYER   Father, may you grant the reader a deeper understanding of the blood covenant through the reading of this chapter. Please reveal the depths of your love in giving your only begotten Son who was slain from the foundation of the world to atone for Adam and Eve's sins and the sins of all mankind. May those who read choose to come into blood covenant with you and gain life eternal.

"And the blood shall be to you for a sign upon the houses where you are. And when I see the blood I will pass over you, and the plague shall not be upon you to destroy you when I smite the land of Egypt."

(Exodus 12:13 NKJV)

"Moses then took the blood, sprinkled it on the people and said, 'This is the blood of the covenant that the Lord has made with you in accordance with all these words.'"

(Exodus 24:8 NIV)

Chapter 2

• •

Blood Traced Through the Old Testament

Blood in the Garden

The scene in the Garden of Eden gives our first glimpse into the importance of the blood. Adam and Eve had sinned! They had disobeyed God in partaking of the fruit of the one tree He had commanded them not to eat. Their sin broke their fellowship with God—their Abba Father and separated them from their Creator cutting off the flow of fellowship between them.

The Lord God (Genesis. 3:21) had made coats of skins and clothed Adam and Eve as described previously in chapter one. The blood associated with these animal sacrifices offered a picture of the blood covering of sin, involving live animals that had been slain. This was a picture of the blood covering of sin, which would be provided by the Lamb of God at Calvary.

Animal Blood Sacrifices

Adam and Eve had probably related this story to their sons, Cain and Abel, thus teaching them the value God placed on animal sacrifices. Abel, in the first recorded act of worship in the Bible, brought fat portions from the first-born of his flock. Cain followed his own inclinations and offered fruit. The Scripture records that *"The Lord looked with favor on Abel and his offering, but on Cain and his offering he did not look with favor"* (Genesis 4:4–5b NIV).

Genesis 15:10–17 states that Abraham took animal sacrifices and divided them through the middle. When the sun went down and it was dark, a smoking fire pot and a burning torch passed between the pieces. The passage of the fire pot and torch represented God's sealing of His covenant promise. In a similar manner common covenants were sealed at that time in history by the parties walking between the split carcasses of animals, which had been specifically killed for the ceremony. This covenanting ritual of passage was as if to say, "This same fate be to all my herds and flocks should I not keep my promise."

Seal of Blood Covenant

Abraham's circumcision, as well as the circumcision of all the men, including his son Ishmael, also sealed Abraham and Sara's covenant with God. This brought the Children of Israel into a blood covenant with God. The seal of the covenant was circumcision on the eighth day of life. *"My covenant in your flesh is to be an everlasting covenant"* (Genesis 17:13b, NIV). The covenant bound Abraham and his descendants by indissoluble ties to Jehovah and it bound Jehovah to Abraham and his descendants.

The only blood of man that God required in Israel was the blood of circumcision. In essence the Hebrew man was giving God his personal blood (life) at the very source of paternity, pledging both himself and those who would come after him in the line of natural descent to Yahweh (Hebrew for God) alone.

Other Examples of Blood Sacrifices/Blood Covenant

Most Christians are familiar with Abraham's obedience to God as he prepared to sacrifice his son of promise, Isaac, on Mt. Moriah. When his hand was stopped, a ram was provided as the blood sacrifice. The great lesson of substitution was revealed here (Genesis. 22:1–18).

Tracing history back to the flood, the first recorded act of Noah after he left the ark was the offering of a burnt sacrifice to God (Genesis. 8:20). Moving forward in Scripture to the exodus out of Egypt, it is recorded that the blood of the lamb was placed on the doorposts of the homes of the Children of Israel. What the blood accomplished on Mt. Moriah for one person, Isaac, was now experienced by the nation of Israel. As they applied the blood to their doorframes (lintels) they were taught that life could be obtained only by the death of a substitute. The Death Angel passed over. They were delivered because they were Abraham's blood covenant descendants. God and Israel were bound together—a blood covenant people. The blood on the doorposts was God's sign of this union. God would not permit the destroyer to enter into the homes of the Israelites in

Egypt. The event stands in history as the Passover. The great destroyer was rendered powerless by the blood (Exodus 12:1–36).

Blood as a Token

When Jericho was conquered by the Israelites, Rahab, the prostitute, was told that her family would be saved if she would hang a scarlet cord from her window as a token of the blood (Joshua 2:17). The spies remembered the blood that had been sprinkled on their doorposts and the deliverance provided by the blood. Exodus 12:13 refers to the blood as a sign. Rahab would have no time to slay an animal when the attack began, so she was to hang a scarlet cord from the window to mark her house. Both the Passover and the story of Rahab are a foreshadowing (picture) of the protection of the blood of Jesus—our Passover Lamb.

When the Children of Israel reached Sinai, God confirmed the covenant as the sacrificial blood was sprinkled on the altar and then on the people. *"Moses then took the blood, sprinkled it on the people and said, 'This is the blood of the covenant that the Lord has made with you in accordance with all these words'"* (Exodus 24:8 NIV). He reserved half the blood to sprinkle on the book of the Covenant. This bound the people to the covenant and bound God to the people. The blood, of course, was a foreshadowing of Jesus' sacrifice, which would be the blood covenant. The first act was a shadow of what was to come. The cross where Jesus shed His blood was the reality. Thank God for the picture of blood sacrifice throughout the Old Testament providing covering or protection and pointing to the supreme blood sacrifice of Jesus, our Lord and Savior.

Blood Traced Through the Old Testament

Blood sacrifices were made in the Old Testament for various reasons, including but not limited to, worship, purification of the people, preparation for battle to invoke God's favor, or as a part of the ritual on special days. Sometimes the sacrifices were for personal sins, sometimes for corporate sin. I have chosen not to include these other types of blood sacrifices, as they are not within the primary focus of this book.

Under the Blood

David Huff

(Verse two)

A perfect plan so long ago—still echoes from a hill,
    whosoever will
Just let him come today—and bring those broken dreams
I know you'll be amazed—with his loving grace
You'll find in Jesus Christ—everything you need
And when the past seems present—
    it's in the sea of forgetfulness
All that I am, and all that I hope to be
I place within your hands
Give me the strength to stand up and walk
And if I stumble, I know you'll understand

Chorus

Thank God I'm over the guilt and shame
Cause I'm under the blood

—David Huff
Huff, Huff, Huff Publishing
Copyright 1995
Used by permission

PRAYER   Father, reveal to your children a deeper understanding of the picture of blood sacrifices presented throughout the Old Testament. Teach them of this foreshadowing of Jesus' sacrifice, which was to come for their own lives.

"In the case of a will, it is necessary to prove the death of the one who made it, because a will is in force only when somebody has died; it never takes effect while the one who made it is living. This is why even the first covenant was not put into effect without blood."

(Hebrews 9:17,18 NIV)

"He did not enter by means of the blood of goats and calves; but he entered the Most Holy Place once for all by his own blood having obtained eternal redemption."

(Hebrews 9:12 NIV)

Chapter 3

. . . .

Parallels in the Old and New Testament

OLD TESTAMENT	NEW TESTAMENT
Sacrifice of animals	Sacrifice of Jesus
Cleansing in outer court	Cleansing at new birth experience
Blood covering right ear, right thumb and big toe of right foot	Our hearing (ear), our works (hand) our daily Christian walk—all covered by the blood
Old Testament priest once a year sacrificed behind the veil	The veil split to provide unrestricted

access to the
Father

| Old Testament priest's sacrifice covered the sin | New Testament High Priest, Jesus, removed sins |

Priesthood

The priests in the Old Testament were from the Tribe of Levi. They offered daily sacrifices for the sins of the people. In addition to daily sin sacrifices, a Day of Atonement called Yom Kippur was observed as a day to cover sins committed during the previous year. The priest would take two he-goats for the nation. One was slain to honor and worship Jehovah. The sins of the people were symbolically laid on the head of the other goat. The animal was the sin-bearer for the nation and was sent into the wilderness. This scape-goat was the foreshadowing of our personal Lord and Savior who became a scapegoat to bear our sins.

One year after the exodus from Egypt, while the Children of Israel were in the Sinai, Moses took the sacrificial blood and sprinkled it on the altar and then on the people. (Exodus 24:8) This act represents the establishment of the covenant between God and the people.

Mark 15:38 tells of the death of Jesus and the rending of the veil at the entrance to the Holy of Holies within the tabernacle. The Holy of Holies was the place the priest carried the blood and sprinkled it upon the mercy seat. "*He did not enter by means of the blood of goats and calves; but he entered the Most Holy Place once for all by his own blood having obtained eternal redemption*" (Hebrews 9:12 NIV). It was

40

a once-for-all sacrifice—the new covenant. Jesus became the guarantee of a better covenant (Hebrews 7:22).

The High Priest

The high priest was an example of the High Priest Christ who was to come. Hebrews 6:19,20 NIV tells us, *"We have this hope as an anchor for the soul, firm and secure. It enters the inner sanctuary behind the curtain, where Jesus, who went before us, has entered on our behalf. He has become a high priest forever, in the order of Melchizedek."*

Our High Priest, Jesus, entered into heaven with His own blood, having obtained eternal redemption for us. When God accepted the blood of Jesus Christ, He signified that the claims of justice had been met. Man could be legally taken from Satan's authority and restored to fellowship with God. Christ's sacrifice had put sin away. He had provided sanctification (purification) for man. He had made it possible for man to be separated from Satan's kingdom.

Symbolism of the Use of the Blood by the Priest

The priest in the Old Testament put blood upon the right ear, right thumb, and great toe of the right foot of the one to be cleansed. The right side throughout the Scriptures is the side of divine favor, and I believe this pictured the favor that man enters into in the new covenant. Jesus' head bled, His hands bled, and His feet bled. This provided for our sanctification in the same corresponding realms of life. The high priest's actions symbolized the blood of Christ that would be in those three places on His body.

The Blood over the Mind

The blood that came from His head reminds us our minds are covered. Victory was provided over troubled, fearful, anxious thoughts. Our minds are the door to our personhood. Just as the blood on the door protected the Children of Israel at Passover, so we can claim the blood over the doorway to our minds. We claim the blood as a barrier to the destroyer when he comes with tormenting thoughts. By faith, we point to the blood and command him to be gone in the name of the Lord Jesus Christ. We believe in and claim the protection of the blood, specifically over our mind. The thoughts are rejected and turned back at the threshold. They are not nursed and allowed to take root. I am indebted to *The Mind Under the Blood* pamphlet, Osterhus Publishing, Minneapolis, MN, for this concept. Many Christians live in defeat because they do not understand that the thought itself is not sin. It is what you do with the thought that is important.

I can testify to the application of this truth in my own life. After an absence of 25 years, I had resumed a nursing career. I was overwhelmed with the masses of paperwork, complex, unfamiliar equipment, and the hectic pace on the cancer ward where I was assigned. At the end of the first exhausting week, I awakened in the night assaulted with thoughts of defeat and despair. "You can't do it, it is too hard, you can't make it, you might as well quit, you have been out of nursing too long." I dragged myself out of bed and went to the living room, feeling tormented by inadequacies. I assumed a prone, face-down prayer posture and started to cry out to the Lord for help. A Scripture

I had committed to memory came to me. *"They overcame him by the blood of the Lamb and the word of their testimony"* (Revelation 12:11 NIV). I started to claim this Scripture and to proclaim it over the situation and myself. After 30 to 45 minutes, I entered into a peace that passed my own understanding. That peace from the Prince of Peace stayed with me no matter what happened during the next nine years. His peace sustained me through the challenges of bedside nursing with cancer patients.

The Reality of Jesus' Blood Sacrifice in the Believer's Christian Walk

The blood of Jesus flowed down and covered His ear. We, by faith, declare that this provides cleansing for what we hear, which then enters into our thought life. The blood of Jesus provides the legal basis for victory in the believer's thought life. We have the mind of Christ through the indwelling Holy Spirit. (Philippians 2:5 NKJV). Our ear is set apart to God so that we can hear our Master's voice. The ear covered by the blood also enables the believer to hear the heart cry of others. As we grow in our spiritual hearing, we learn to receive promptings of the Holy Spirit on specific ways to minister to others.

Jesus' hands were nailed and blood came forth. We remember that the Old Testament priest put blood on the thumb of the right hand. This symbolizes the ministry He calls us to. The work of our hands is covered by the blood. This was pictured in the Old Testament by the priest and became a reality as Jesus hung on the cross.

The blood was put on the big toe of the right foot of the Israelites as a picture. Jesus' feet were nailed and bled so that His precious blood might be upon our walk with the Father. Jesus' feet were nailed so that our feet might walk in unrestricted fellowship with the Father. The blood of Jesus Christ provides a basis for continual walking in fellowship as we stay in a cleansed position by quickly repenting as He shows us areas that are not in line with His godly standards.

After an Israelite was anointed in the three specific areas, the oil was poured all over the head and coursed down his garments. This represents the fullness of the Holy Spirit upon the believer. Another interesting fact to consider is that on the Day of Atonement blood was sprinkled on the book that contained the law of God. Sprinkling the blood upon a written record bound God to His word. Then Moses sprinkled all the people with blood. This bound Israel to the covenant by the blood. God was joined to Israel by the blood.

Scripture says we are priests! (1 Peter 2:9, Revelation 1:6). We are to minister to God's creation on the earth. This, of course, is done through the power of the indwelling Holy Spirit. We know that our High Priest, Jesus, is seated at the right hand of God the Father. He ever lives to intercede for us (Romans 8:34).

What Can Wash Away My Sins?

What can wash away my sin? Nothing but the blood of Jesus;
What can make me whole again? Nothing but the blood of Jesus.

For my pardon this I see—Nothing but the blood of Jesus
For my cleansing this my plea—Nothing but the blood
of Jesus
Nothing can for sin atone—Nothing but the blood of Jesus.

Naught of good that I have done—Nothing but the blood
of Jesus

Chorus

O precious is the flow that makes me white as snow;
No other fount I know, nothing but the blood of Jesus.

Robert Lowry
Great Songs of the Church—Number Two
Standard Publishing

PRAYER   Father, grant us the grace, vision and understanding to lay hold of the blood provision Jesus
made for our Christian walk and ministry.

I had lived through a very serious depression with my close
friend. We had tried every thing in the natural and in the spiritual and had seen deliverance from a spirit of suicide.

We had many other wonderful answers to prayer. As
the months went on and the depression did not totally lift,
I confess to becoming agitated with the situation and nag-
ging the Lord in prayer. I went over the same requests time
and time again. Finally, the Lord spoke to my heart to fast
and pray for a period of time with the conviction that a

further level of deliverance from Satan's harassment would be accomplished. During this time I recorded many prayers and claimed many Scripture passages over her. These included the Lord's Prayer, the 23rd Psalm, the Beatitudes, Psalms 91, the Ten Commandments, and numerous other Scriptures. He led me to scriptural truths in Christian books, which I also prayed over her. At the end of this time, I held up the notebook containing the 30 pages I had recorded and asked the Father to send the Holy Spirit to blow over the bowl of prayers that had been said over her by myself and many others for a number of years. I asked that the petitions and proclamations would come up as a sweet aroma in the nostrils of God the Father—a great rendering of prayer on her behalf.

I experienced a tremendous relief by following a technique I learned in a book *The Confident Woman* by Anabel Gillham. I took a helium balloon with a long string attached, which I wrapped loosely around a brick. The balloon represents the burden you are releasing to the Lord. Mrs. Gillham suggests writing the problem you are trying to release on the balloon, but my problem was too big. I held it straight out in front of me until my arm was exhausted from the weight of the brick. I dropped the brick and the balloon floated off. It was an emotional moment when it lifted higher and higher and disappeared into the clouds. I heard in my spirit, "You have not released her to Satan, you have released her to Me." This gave me a picture of relinquishment of a very troublesome situation where I was guilty of the sin of worry.

After this, whenever I started to repeat the many prayers said in her behalf, I would be prompted in my spirit, "No, you have already said that, just pray the blood." This happened over and over as He trained me in a new level of trust. For one year I declared my friend to be in the blood covenant. I prayed very little else except as new specific situations arose I felt released to lift them up. Over that year I saw a remarkable change for which I praise His name. She became much calmer, less agitated, and her healing continues to manifest.

"Surely he took up our infirmities and carried our sorrows, yet we considered him stricken by God, smitten by him, and afflicted. But he was pierced for our transgressions, he was crushed for our iniquities; the punishment that brought us peace was upon him and by his wounds we are healed."

(Isaiah 53:4,6 NIV)

"To Him Who loved us and washed us from our sins in His own blood."

(Revelation 1:5b NKJV)

Chapter 4

· ·

Crucifixion: Significance of Jesus' Wounds

Precious Blood

Words and music by Lanny Wolfe. © 1980 Lanny Wolfe Music. All rights controlled by Gaither copyright Management. Used by permission

So many years so many lambs were offered up.
For all the blood that was spilled could never fill that
bitter cup.
Till one spotless lamb in the form of man gave His life
on Calvary.
His was the only blood that could ever set me free.

Chorus

For His blood was not just blood of another spotless lamb,
But His blood was precious blood for it washed my sins
away,
And His blood it heals my body and it sets my spirit free,
And I'm so glad His precious blood still flows from
Calvary.

No other blood could heal my broken body
And no other blood could save my sin sick soul
And no other blood could conquer death and win the
victory.
No other blood but the blood Jesus shed for me

Oh, and His blood it heals my body and it sets my spirit
free,
And I'm so glad this precious blood, yes, I'm so glad this
precious blood
His blood heals my body and sets my spirit free,
I'm so glad this precious blood still flows from Calvary.

God Came Down

Our Lord and Savior Jesus Christ was divine love incarnated. God came down to earth in the form of a man. He literally gave of Himself to make provision for the fall of the first man, Adam. Scripture speaks of Jesus as the last Adam. He came and offered a way for the effects of Adam and Eve's poor choice (disobedience to God) to be reversed. The Bible refers to Jesus as the Lamb of God who was slain from the foundation of the world (Revelation 13:8).

Hebrews 9:22 NKJV states, *"According to the law almost all things are purified with blood, and without the shedding of blood there is no remission."* The blood sacrifice to cover the sins of the world flowed out of Jesus' body at the cross. He gave His perfect blood as an offering to cover the sins of any man, woman or child who would avail themself of His offering.

Jesus' head bled as the crown of thorns was forced down in anger on His holy brow. His side bled as the spear pierced it. His hands bled as the nails were hammered into them. His feet bled as the nails went in. His back bled as the whip was used to scourge Him. Jesus Christ's body contained a fountain of blood that was sealed until the day His skin was pierced. When the skin of His body was punctured, the fountain was opened; it flowed then, it flows now in the spirit realm by faith, and it will flow until eternity! He is the source of the cleansing stream that washes away our sins. *"To Him who loved us and washed us from our sins in His own blood"* (Revelation 1:5b NKJV).

In 1 Corinthians 15:45 NLT *"The Scriptures tell us, the first man, Adam, became a living person. But the last Adam, that is Christ—is a life giving Spirit."*

It is interesting to look back and remember that the high priest in the Old Testament (described in Chapter Three) applied blood to the right ear, thumb of the right hand and the big toe of the right foot of the one to be cleansed. This was reenacted in Jesus as His head bled, His hands bled, and His feet bled. This provided for our sanctification in the same corresponding realms of life. The high priest's actions symbolized the blood of Christ that would correspond to the same three areas of Jesus' body.

The Mind and the Ear Covered by the Blood

The blood that came from His head reminds us our minds are covered. Man's mind is the gateway to his threefold being. An ungodly thought comes to the threshold of our mind. If we allow it in, it leads to sin and shame. We entertain doubt, anxiety and nervousness. Our physical and spiritual rest is disrupted. 2 Corinthians 10:4,5 NIV states, *"The weapons we fight with are not the weapons of the world. On the contrary they have divine power to demolish strongholds. We demolish arguments and every pretension that sets itself up against the knowledge of God and we take captive every thought to make it obedient to Christ."*

The ear is the source of outside distractions. What comes in through the ear gate enters the mind and influences our thoughts and actions. We think back to the door in Egypt with the blood sprinkled over and around it. Exodus 12:21–24 teaches us that the destroyer could not get in. In the same way we, by faith, claim the blood over our minds—the doorway to our personhood. We claim, believe, and experience by faith the blood of Jesus over and around our minds. Just as the door to the physical house of the Israelites was protected by the blood, so we have divine help for our thought life. We claim the blood is over the door—the door to our minds. Our minds are influenced by what comes into our ear from others, from Satan as he injects lies, often mixed with some truth, or by what we say to ourselves. As we claim the blood over our minds and ears we can be free of torment and distractions. By faith, Jesus' blood covers our minds. We are protected as we declare our faith in the provision of Jesus' blood to cover our thoughts.

While working with a freelance editor on the proposal for this book, I was bombarded with discouragement. I had been writing for about two years and had had several articles published, but Satan was trying to undermine me in carrying out the assignment the Lord had given me. I was to write a book on the blood of Jesus. The suggestions I was receiving from the editor seemed overwhelming to implement and my computer continued to be a challenge with my limited computer skills. The deadline for the proposal was fast approaching. Discouragement was nipping at my mind as I once again faced numerous revisions. I assumed my emergency prayer position (prone face down) and started asking the Lord for help, declaring that I am a blood covenant woman. I have the mind of Christ. I can do all things through Christ who gives me the strength. I started focusing on Him and His resources confessing my discouragement and frustration with the situation.

I prayed and "snuggled" down into His presence, confessing that I am covered by the blood and I am His child. The attack lifted! I arose and went immediately with excitement to face the challenge of yet another revision of the material selected for the proposal.

My friend's Christian father-in-law (who has Alzheimer's) was uncooperative and belligerent. This was causing difficulty for Drew as the primary care giver. She followed a suggestion to lay hands on him and pray with him. He was agreeable. She proclaimed aloud the power of the blood covenant over him especially over his mind. Drew continued this proclamation daily, that, as a believer, Grandpa Jim has a blood covering over him. He became cooperative, willing to take his medication, go for walks, and submit to care in general. He became much calmer and less agitated. After three months of marked improvement, a bed opened up in a nursing home near Drew's home. She and her husband felt this was the Lord's provision for Grandpa Jim. He readily cooperated with the decision to move and is happy in the new environment.

His improved behavior continues as the nurses report he willingly takes his medication and complies in general with the routine. Drew continues to use the spoken aloud declaration of the power of the blood over this precious family member.

The blood of Jesus flowed down from His head and covered His ears. This pictures the provision of cleansing from what we hear which is then taken into our thought life. As stated earlier, the blood of Jesus provides the legal basis for victory in the believer's thought life (1 Corinthians 2:16b NIV) *"But we have the mind of Christ."* Our ears are set apart as they are covered by the blood. We are promised that we can hear our shepherd's voice (John 10:1–16).

Hands Covered by the Blood

Jesus' hands were nailed and blood flowed. The Old Testament priest put blood on the thumb of the right hand. This symbolizes that the blood covers the work of our hands as we carry out the ministry He gives us. The covering was pictured by the priest, enacted on the cross and is now available to every believer by faith.

Christian's Walk Covered by the Blood

The blood was placed on the big toe of the right foot in the Old Testament. Jesus' feet were nailed and bled so that His precious blood might be upon our walk with the Father. Jesus' feet were nailed so we could walk in fellowship as we avail ourselves of continual cleansing.

After the priests anointed the person in the three specific areas we have discussed, the oil was poured over his head and the excess ran down his clothes. This was a picture of the provision of the Holy Spirit for the believer.

Jesus' Gift Through His Sacrifice

The stripes placed on Jesus' back are referred to in the Gospels as flogging. Isaiah 53:4,5 NKJV—"*Surely He has borne our griefs And carried our sorrows; Yet we esteemed Him stricken, Smitten by God, and afflicted. But He was wounded for our transgressions, He was bruised for our iniquities; The chastisement for our peace was upon Him. And by His stripes we are healed.*" God foreknew the fall of man and He had planned the stripes that would provide the means by which Jesus would bear the sins and sicknesses of mankind.

When Jesus' side was pierced, a fountain of blood was opened. Zechariah spoke of it in chapter 3 verse 9b. "*I will remove the iniquity of that land in one day*" (NKJV). Jesus is the source of the cleansing stream that washes away our sins. Revelation 1:5b NKJV—"*To Him who loved us and washed us from our sins in His own blood.*" Jesus' side was pierced and some believe His heart ruptured under the agony of the sins of the world, past, present, and yet to be committed. The sacrifice of animal lambs in the Old Testament was a picture of the sacrifice, which was to come of Jesus, the Lamb of God. *"We all like sheep, have gone astray, each of us has turned to his own way and the Lord has laid on him the iniquity of us all"* (Isaiah 53:6 NIV). The figure of a lamb is a picture of sacrifice throughout the Old Testament.

The chastisement of our peace was upon Him (Isaiah 53:5). This precious blood is to be used for overcoming Satan in warfare. Jesus won the victory at the cross and the resurrection. We enforce the victory by faith as we declare the blood covers us. The atoning blood is our weapon against sin and Satan as we withstand temptations from within and temptations coming from outside ourselves.

There is a Fountain Filled with Blood

There is a fountain filled with blood
drawn from Emmanuel's veins;
And sinners, plunged beneath that flood,
Lose all their guilty stains.

The dying thief rejoiced to see
That fountain in his day;
And there may I, though sinful, too,
wash all my sins away,

Dear dying Lamb,
Thy precious blood shall
Never lose its power,
'Til all the ransomed Church of God
Be saved, to sin no more,

And since, by faith, I saw the stream
Thy flowing wounds supply,
Redeeming love has been my theme,
And shall be 'til I die. Amen

William Cowper/William Gardiner
Great Songs of the Church—Number Two
Standard Publishing

PRAYER   Father, imprint upon our spirits the reality
of the supreme sacrifice of Jesus. Help us to
walk out the daily provision He made for us
to live in victory in our thought life.

"For God was pleased to have all his fullness dwell in him, and through Him to reconcile to himself all things on earth or things in heaven, by making peace through his blood, shed on the cross."

(Colossians 1:19,20 NIV)

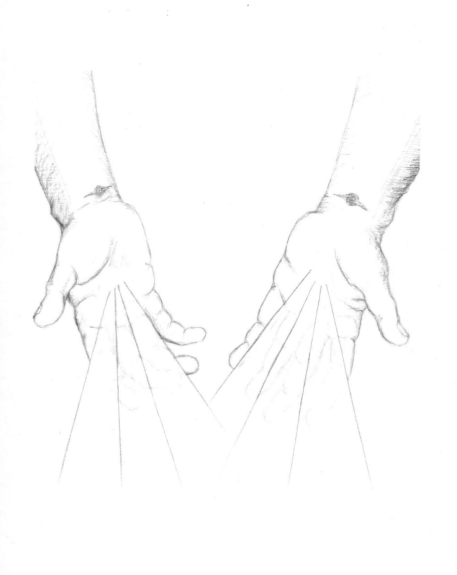

"But if we walk in the light, as he is in the light, we have fellowship with one another, and the blood of Jesus, his Son, purifies us from every sin."

(1 John 1:7 NIV)

Chapter 5

The Physical and Spiritual Functions and Benefits of the Blood

*J*esus often taught by parables—a way of looking at something in the natural to illustrate a spiritual truth. It is interesting to consider the blood in this way.

PHYSICAL

1. **Removes waste**
   We know that the blood circulates and carries waste from the body.

2. **Supplies life**
   The blood carries life (oxygen and nutrients) to the millions of body cells.

SPIRITUAL

1. **The blood of Jesus**
   Cleanses us as we confess our sins. 1 John 1:9 NIV *"If we confess our sins, he is faithful and just and will forgive us our sins and purify us from all unrighteousness."*

2. **Abundant life** is in Him.
   John 10:10b NKJV *"I am come that they may have life and they may have it more **abundantly.**"*

3. **Temperature**
Warms body, the blood circulates through the body maintaining the temperature.

3. **Spiritual Zeal**
Maintains spiritual climate control. Helps us stay on fire. Remembering all that the blood has accomplished will help us obey. Romans 12:11 NIV *"Never be lacking in zeal, but keep your spiritual fervor, serving the Lord."*

4. **Energizes**
Infuses energy through oxygen and nutrients.

4. **Spiritual recharging**
We are spiritually energized as we stay close to the Father who provided the blood covenant, drawing on His strength. Hebrews 10:19 NIV *"Therefore, brothers, since we have confidence to enter the Most Holy Place by the blood of Jesus . . ."*

5. **First Aid in emergencies**
When we are in an emergency situation the blood rushes to supply adrenaline and hormones and clots to stop bleeding.

5. **Spiritual emergencies**
Revelation 12:11a NIV *"They overcame him by the blood of the lamb."* We claim the power of Jesus' blood (which represents His life force) over us in spiritual crisis.

6. **Defensive force**
The blood provides defense against infectious agents and attacks against our body.

6. **Spiritual defense**
Jesus' blood provides divine protection for the believer from the attacks of Satan.

7. **Proper environment**
The blood supplies the fluid to maintain the proper atmosphere for the cells of our body.

7. **Spiritual climate**
The blood provides the believer with the legal entry into God's presence.

The author is indebted to Marilyn Hickey's booklet *The Power of the Blood, A Physician's Analysis* for many of the concepts in the material comparing the natural and spiritual parallels of the blood.

As believers proclaiming the blood, we are calling on the life of Jesus to penetrate the situation we are offering up in petition. The applied blood of Jesus has the power, by faith, to cleanse and remove the waste—the garbage in our lives. We have divine protection through the shed blood of Jesus.

My friend, Linda told me a story of the miraculous deliverance of her son, which illustrates being delivered out of the hand of the enemy. Linda was in the habit of declaring the blood covenant provisions over each of her children on a regular basis. John was attending a birthday party in New York City when he felt an impending sense of danger. He gathered the five other boys who came with him saying, "This is not the place we need to be." As they were going to their vehicle two other boys followed them out of the party and one pulled out a gun demanding all of their "shine" (expensive jewelry). John and his friends quickly got into the vehicle following John's instructions to "hit the floor." Two shots hit the passenger side door. Anticipating the next bullet, John hunched over on the seat between his long legs. The bullet that was intended for his head lodged in his leg where it remains trouble free to this day several years later.

Then miraculously the gun jammed! John remembers praying, "Lord, I am in deep trouble, I need to have great wisdom to know what to do." He was impressed to put the gear in reverse and then forward rocking the vehicle. John told his mother that the cars blocking his exit just seemed to part providing a passageway for him to drive rapidly away avoiding further attack. As amazing as it seems there was an ambulance just a short distance away attending a heart attack victim. The paramedics were able to quickly stop the bleeding from John's knee and call another ambulance to transport him to the hospital. The dr. told him there was no permanent damage to his knee; if he had to be shot it was the best place. The bullet was left in the tissue of the knee because of the damage it would cause to remove it.

Another friend, Becky, told me this story. "Early in the morning, five days a week, I walk from my home to a neighborhood park on a walking path. I use the 3–4 mile walk as a time of praise, meditation, and prayer. After reaching the park and circling it twice, I sit on a bench in a quiet, secluded area, take communion, and apply the precious blood of Jesus for protection over every aspect of the lives of my family and myself—everything that may confront us or that may affect us in any way that day.

One morning, having had communion and leaving the park to return home, I passed a house that had a practically new, discarded piece of 2x4 wood, about the size I had planned to buy to nail in my closet. I picked it up and walked on, holding it like a cane. I had only gone 4–5 houses down the street when a lady came out her front door with a dog on a leash. Seeing me, the dog broke loose from her, completely ignoring her screams and attempts to regrasp the leash. He came at me, seemingly intent on having me for breakfast. All his white teeth were bared as he circled me several times trying to get to me. I was able to defend my-self with the piece of wood (symbolic of the provision of the applied blood of Jesus). When the lady was finally able to retrieve the leash, the dog continued to lunge at me. It took all her effort and strength to hold him back. I calmly walked away. In all truth I can say, that although I felt the need to use the 2x4, the source of defense that God had chosen to provide for me after I had proclaimed the mighty blood covering, I never felt any fear or terror. As I was walking home, I decided the 2x4 was thicker than I wanted so I discarded it at the street in front of my house."

Redeemed

1.) Through the blood of Jesus I am **redeemed (delivered and saved)** out of the hand of the devil. *"Let the redeemed of the Lord say so whom He has redeemed from the hand of the enemy"* (Psalms 107:2 NKJV).

Cleansed

2.) Through the blood of Jesus I am **continually cleansed from sin**. *"But if we walk in the light, as he is in the light, we have fellowship with one another and the blood of Jesus, his Son, purifies us from all sin"* (1 John 1:7 NIV).

Justified

3.) Through the blood of Jesus I am **justified (vindicated)**. *"Much more then, having been justified by His blood, we shall be saved from wrath through Him"* (Romans 5:9 NKJV).

Sanctified

4.) Through the blood of Jesus I am **sanctified (purified)**, set apart to a sacred purpose. *"Therefore Jesus also, that He might sanctify the people with His own blood suffered outside the gate"* (Hebrews 13:12 NKJV).

Reconciled

5.) Through the blood of Jesus I am **reconciled (brought in harmony with/made right) to God**. *"For if, when we were enemies we were reconciled to God through the death of His Son, much more, having been reconciled, we shall be saved by His life. And not only that, but we also rejoice in God through our Lord Jesus Christ, through whom we have now received reconciliation"* (Romans 5:10–11 NKJV).

Access to Holy of Holies

6.) Through the blood of Jesus I **gain entrance to the Holy of Holies**. *"Therefore, brethren, having boldness to enter the Holiest by the blood of Jesus . . ."* (Hebrews 10:19 NKJV). The moment Jesus released His spirit as He hung on the cross the curtain enclosing the Holy of Holies in the temple was torn in two from top to bottom. God's presence, which had been open only to the High Priest, was now open to any person who would receive Jesus' sacrifice as an offering for his sins.

Clear Conscience

7.) Through the blood of Jesus I am set **free from oppression of an evil conscience.**

> *"For if the blood of bulls and goats and the ashes of a heifer, sprinkling the unclean, sanctifies for the purifying of the flesh, how much more shall the blood of Christ, who through the eternal Spirit offered Himself without spot to God, cleanse your conscience from dead works to serve the living God?"*
>
> (Hebrews 9:13,14 NKJV)

Have You Been to Jesus?

Have you been to Jesus for the cleansing power?
Are you washed in the blood of the Lamb?
Are you fully trusting in His grace this hour?
Are you washed in the blood of the Lamb?
Are you walking daily by the Savior's side?
Are you washed in the blood of the Lamb?
Do you rest each moment in the crucified?
Are you washed in the blood of the Lamb?
When the Bridegroom cometh will your robes be white,
Pure and white in the blood of the Lamb?
Will your soul be ready for the mansions bright?
And be washed in the blood of the Lamb?
Lay aside the garments that are stained with sin,
And be washed in the blood of the Lamb;
There's a fountain flowing for the soul unclean:
O be washed in the blood of the Lamb?

The Power of the Lamb's Blood

Chorus

Are you washed in the blood, in the soul-cleansing blood
   of the Lamb?
Are your garments spotless? Are they white as snow?
Are you washed in the blood of the Lamb?

E.A. Hoffman
Great Songs of the Church—Number Two
Standard Publishing

PRAYER   Father; grant us a deeper appreciation of what you provided for us at the cross. Grant to us a great inner swelling of gratitude beyond anything we have experienced before. Seal in our hearts a deep thankfulness for the gift of your Son.

"For by one man's disobedience many were made sinners, so also by one man's obedience many will be made righteous."

(Romans 5:19 NKJV)

*"Through him and for his name's sake, we received grace
and apostleship to call people from all the Gentiles to the
obedience that comes from faith."*

(Romans 1:5 NIV)

Chapter 6

. . . .

The Importance of Obedience

Sin Nature Passed Down

The disobedience of Adam and Eve resulted in destruction and havoc that continues to daily plague mankind even into the 21ˢᵗ century. An inroad was given to Satan to afflict God's creation. Adam and Eve listened to Satan, the father of lies, (John 4:44) and their action resulted in an erosion of their physical and spiritual bond with their Creator. Scripture tells us the sins of the fathers are visited to the third and fourth generation. It is clear that we come under a penalty because of family sin. *"The Lord is long suffering and abundant in mercy, forgiving iniquity and transgressions: but He by no means **clears** the guilty, visiting the iniquity of the fathers on the children to the third and fourth generation"* (Numbers 14:18 NKJV).

Obedience at Passover

The preparation for the great exodus out of Egypt is known in history as the Passover. In this we are taught the importance of obedience. The head of the family was responsible for offering a spotless, unblemished animal that was put to death as a sin sacrifice. The blood of the animal was caught in a basin and applied to the doorposts of the dwellings with hyssop (thought to be an herb used for purifying). Obedience to instructions provided deliverance from the destroyer who passed through claiming the life of every firstborn son who was not inside a dwelling marked with (protected by) the blood. Exodus 11 and 12 recount the event. Obedience was required in observing the Passover instructions with the father being held accountable for applying the protection for his household. Staying inside the houses covered by the blood protected the Israelites. A firstborn son would have suffered the same fate as an Egyptian had they disobeyed and come out from behind the blood covering.

Jesus' Example of Obedience

Jesus Christ (the believer's Passover lamb) was a perfect pattern of obedience. He said, *"For I have not spoken on My own authority; but the Father who sent Me gave Me a command, what I should say and what I should speak"* (John 12:49 NKJV).

Hebrews 5:8–9 NLT tells us, *"So even though Jesus was God's Son, he learned obedience from the things he suffered. In this way, God qualified him as a perfect High Priest, and he became the source of eternal salvation for all those who obey* him." Philippians 2:8 NKJV states, "*And being found in appearance as a man, He humbled Himself and became obedient to the point of death, even the death of the cross.*"

Romans 5:19 NKJV shows the contrast between Adam and Jesus Christ. "*For by one man's disobedience many were made sinners, so also by one Man's obedience many will be made righteous.*"

The believer in Christ is encouraged with "*Through him and for his name's sake, we received grace and apostleship to call people from all the Gentiles to the obedience that comes from faith*" (Romans 1:5 NIV).

Deuteronomy 11:13–32 and Deuteronomy 28 give in great detail the blessings of being obedient as promised to the Children of Israel.

EXODUS 19:5 refers to those who obey God as "*a special treasure to me above all people.*" Revelation 22:14 NKJV states: "*Blessed are those who do His commandments that they may have the right to the tree of life, and may enter through the gates into the city.*"

Believer's Call to Obedience

In contemplation of obedience, we know there are lines of authority to which Scripture commands us to be subject (Romans 13:1, Ephesians. 5:22–25). These commandments are given to the entire body of Christ in Scripture. The believer has to seek the Lord when he is confronted with various interpretations. In addition, each believer has specific areas in his life that the Lord God wants to bring in line with His holy standards. The believer has the indwelling Holy Spirit as teacher and as prompter. Our challenge and privilege is to obey those promptings, being sure to test them against Godly principles and Scripture.

It is essential that we, as believers, keep a clean slate with God. When we become aware of having sinned, we need to be quick to follow 1 John 1:9 NLT. *"But if we confess our sins to him, he is faithful and just to forgive us and to cleanse us from every wrong."*

Our blood protection is a hedge that guards us on every side. Our hedge of protection ensures us of continual blessing from God unless we **tear** down the hedge by disobedience.

"He who digs a pit will fall into it. And whoever breaks through a wall will be bitten by a serpent" (Ecclesiastes 10:8 NKJV).

Praise God our sins were washed away at our salvation experience by Jesus' blood sacrifice. When God sees the blood, He does not see sin. When we confess our sins we are immediately received back into right relationship with our heavenly Father. Sometimes, however, there are consequences of sin with which we must deal. The Bible gives some beautiful verses on God's attitude towards the sins of His children. We need to be reminded of these so our enemy cannot torment us over confessed sins. We can and should be pleased to walk in the freedom God's word promises.

"I, even I, am He who blots out your transgressions for my own sake, and I will not remember your sins."

(Isaiah 43:25 NKJV)

"He has not dealt with us according to our sins, Nor punished us according to our iniquities. For as the heavens are high above the earth, So great is His mercy toward those

who fear Him. As far as the east is from the west so far has He removed our transgressions from us."

(Psalms 103:10–12 NKJV)

"Who is a God like you who pardons sin and forgives the transgression of the remnant of his inheritance? You do not stay angry forever but delight to show mercy. You will again have compassion on us; you will tread our sins underfoot and hurl our iniquities into the depths of the sea."

(Micah 7:18–19 NIV)

Another great promise is found in Isaiah 38:17 NIV. *"Surely it was for my benefit that I suffered such anguish. In your love you kept me from the pit of destruction, you have put all my sins behind your back."*

The adversary, Satan, tempts us to disobedience that we might break our hedge. The believer who does not rule well over his own life is like a city without defenses. He has no protection from satanic invasion. *"Whoever has no rule over his own spirit is like a city broken down without walls"* (Proverbs 25:28 NKJV).

A friend of mine told me of a test of obedience in her antebellum country home in Kentucky. The heat in the rambling rooms is controlled by individual breakers. Returning from a trip, Sara found the kitchen cold and went to the basement to reset the breaker. In about five minutes the heat went off again. She repeated this resetting of the breaker two more times with the same results. On the third time she said to the Lord, "Our money is your money, if you want us to use it to call someone to fix this O.K. But I would rather you would show me what to do. You have the wisdom; you know what to do. I am calling on your character and nature to show me what to do as I am your blood covenant child." As she walked away she felt a prompting to turn off all the breakers and turn them back on again. She disregarded the prompting and started back upstairs again. As she did so the Lord spoke to her spirit, "If you ask me what to do and don't obey me I will not be pleased and I may not be as quick to answer you next time you ask for help." Repentantly, she returned to the breakers, shut them all off, reset them, and went upstairs. The problem was solved with no further trouble. Later someone told her this is a known step in dealing with this problem.

Jesus Keep Me Near the Cross

Jesus, keep me near the cross; there a precious fountain,
Free to all, a healing stream, flows from Calv'ry's
  mountain.
Near the cross, a trembling soul, love and mercy found me;
There the bright and Morning Star sheds its beams
  around me.
Near the cross! Oh Lamb of God; bring its scenes before
  me;
Help me walk from day to day with its shadow o'er me.

Chorus

In the cross, in the cross, is my glory ever.
Till my raptured soul shall find rest beyond the river.

Fanny J. Crosby, W.H. Doane
Great Songs of the Church—Number Two
Standard Publishing

PRAYER   Father, draw us so into your love that we will faithfully cultivate a lifestyle of quickly obeying you, as we perceive your voice and your will. Empower us to be obedient even unto death.

"Be shepherds of the church of God which he bought with his own blood."

(Acts 20:28b NIV)

"To him who loves us and has freed us from our sins by his blood, and has made us to be a kingdom and priests to serve his God and Father—to him be glory and power for ever and ever. Amen."

(Revelation 1:5b,6 NIV)

Chapter 7

. . . .

Standing in Victory and Celebrating the Victory

Divine Love Expressed

*J*esus expressed a magnificent act of love as He went to the cross, embracing the will of His Father. He took the punishment for the sins of mankind on Himself as He endured pain, torture and suffering. An eternal source of Holy blood from the perfect, unblemished Lamb of God was opened for all who will receive it by faith.

Deliverance from Satan

The blood of Jesus Christ is the foundation for the believer's salvation. Jesus' blood conquered Satan and provided the means for the believer to live with God forever in eternity. It also provides ongoing deliverance from the ravages of sin. We have a vicious enemy who *"prowls around like a roaring lion looking for someone to devour"* (1 Peter 5:8b NIV). Satan hopes we do not know and understand our kingdom inheritance. We have to remind him we are blood bought and washed, and our sins are removed as we confess them and walk in the light. 1 John 1:7 NIV assures us, *"But if we walk in the light, as He is in the light we have fellowship one with another, and the blood of Jesus, His Son, purifies us from every sin."* We overcome the enemy by the provision of our Father when we proclaim aloud the benefits of the blood. We come to our place of service in God's kingdom with the power of our victory over Satan gained by Jesus' death. We march on, and no power of the enemy is able to stand against us.

Each believer is to bear witness to the atoning sacrifice of Jesus Christ and its power to save mankind. *"Let the redeemed of the Lord say so, Whom He hath redeemed from the hand of the enemy"* (Psalms 107:2 NKJV). We are redeemed from the hand of the enemy. We must remind our enemy of that truth and enforce it by the *audibly spoken* word of Scripture.

A friend of mine shared a powerful story with me about her mother who was a praying woman. This mother claimed the protection of the blood covenant over her daughter daily. One Sunday, Edna's mother laid hands on her and claimed the blood as a protection over her as she left for work. Part of Edna's summer job was traveling every Sunday in a small private plane with her boss, a physician, to provide medical care to indigent people.

After they had completed the day's work, Edna and her boss were driven to the open field to fly home. While taxiing through the tall grass, the plane's tire suddenly hit a huge rock, causing the plane to flip over a couple of times, eventually landing upside down. Edna was trapped under the pilot's seat. She was drenched with gasoline. The man who had driven Edna and her boss to the airstrip saw the accident, quickly got out of his truck, and ax in hand, freed Edna and the physician. As they walked away, the plane burst into flames and blew up. Edna's mother told her later that she had felt a real urgency to pray for her at the exact time of the accident.

This story encourages us to be steadfast in prayer for the protection of others as well as for ourselves. The blood is a mighty force of protection as the believer declares his faith in the blood of Jesus.

Just as the high priest in the Old Testament took a basin of blood physically into the inner court, the Holy of Holies, (to sprinkle for the sins of the people), so we, by faith, symbolically take the blood of Jesus and sprinkle it on situations in our lives and those around us by the word of our testimony. We declare we are blood-covenant children. We take the blood, by faith, from the cross and verbally proclaim its power in our daily lives.

The life of Jesus is in the blood, as all life is in the blood. (Leviticus. 17:11) When we, by faith, call on the power of the blood we are calling for the life of Jesus to come to bear on the situation facing us. The Children of Israel applied the blood with the hyssop to their door posts. We, as believers, receive the blood covering over our hearts (the doorway to our personhood) when we experience the new birth. Then we become responsible for claiming the benefits Scripture promises us. Revelation 12:11 NIV declares, *"They overcame him (Satan) by the blood of the lamb and by the word of their testimony."* The word of our testimony is our hyssop.

It is what we use to declare the blood over an individual situation to cause the power of the blood to come to bear on the need that is present.

Blood Cry of the Believer

When we call on the blood we cry for mercy from the mercy seat in heaven where Jesus is seated with the Father—His Father—our Father. The whole realm of God's power is opened when the child of God honors, uses, and audibly claims the blood of Jesus. There is a royal bloodline, and the great destroyer cannot get through it.

We must remember to appropriate the blood by speaking its benefits in faith in the name of the Lord Jesus Christ. It is *not a passive faith* in the blood that brings victory. It is an *active proclaiming of faith*. But proclaiming the blood of Jesus without obedience to the Word of God will avail us nothing! Disobedience breaks the bloodline and allows Satan entrance into the circumstances affecting our lives.

Drawing on the Blood Provision

Looking back to the Old Testament, priests applied blood to those to whom he was ministering. This figuratively is a picture that the blood will cleanse and sanctify all that enters into our ear, everything we put our hand to, and covers every path our foot treads upon during the course of our daily walk.

Exodus 12:24 NKJV says in referring to the application of the blood on the door posts: "*And you shall observe this thing as an ordinance to you and your sons forever.*" Hebrews.

9:12 tells us Jesus went once for all into the Holy of Holies with His own blood to secure a complete redemption—everlasting release for us. We have the benefits of His blood sacrifice available to us. Yet, it is the believer's privilege to draw on this deposit. Just as we write a check to draw out of our financial bank account, we must also draw on the spiritual bank of benefits of the blood by speaking in faith. The hyssop available to us today is the declaration with our mouth as we draw on the provision made possible by the blood. Just as the Children of Israel used the hyssop to apply the blood to their doorposts, we must speak the blood promises over our concerns. We are calling for the power of Jesus Christ to come to bear on the situation.

A lady told me that when she was eight years old she had rheumatism in her knees. Her mother felt led to set a day aside to fast and pray, pleading the blood over her child. At the end of the day she laid hands on her young child and prayed for her healing claiming the power of the blood. The next day the affliction was completely gone and has never returned.

Often we must battle with unseen demonic forces before we can get answers to our prayers. Proclaiming the blood will confound the opposing evil spiritual forces that often delay God's answers. Declaring the authority of the blood of Jesus has a primary place in all intercessory prayer.

Power in the Blood

The life of Jesus is in His blood. When we point to the blood sacrifice provided by Jesus Christ at the cross, we are calling on the power of His life to come to bear on the situations we face. Each time we proclaim, in faith, the power of the blood, we are bringing the life force of Jesus Christ to bear upon whatever crisis is at hand. We claim and proclaim the blood of Jesus and command Satan to loose his grip in the name of Jesus. We always remember that it is the indwelling Holy Spirit who gives us strength to do this. It is not rote, fleshly chanting or ritual. It is the blood-bought child of Father God standing boldly and confidently in the gracious salvation provided at the cross by the shed blood of the Lamb of God.

Revelation 5:9 NKJV speaks of the twenty-four elders in heaven falling down before the Lamb: "*And they sang a new song: 'You are worthy to take the scroll, And to open its seals; For you were slain, And with your blood you purchased men for God from every tribe and language and people and nation. You made them be a kingdom and priests to serve our God and they will reign on the earth.'*" Hebrews 10:19 NIV states, "*Therefore brothers, since we have confidence to enter the most Holy place by the blood of Jesus, by a new and living way opened for us through the curtain, that is his Body, and since we have a great priest over the house of God, let us draw near to God with a sincere heart in full assurance of faith, having our hearts sprinkled to cleanse us from a guilty conscience and having our bodies washed with pure water.*" This verse makes clear we are to have full confidence to enter the Holy of Holies (the interior portion of the Old Testament tabernacle symbolizing, for the present day believer, the place closest to God) by the power and virtue of the blood. Hebrews 4:16 AMP states, "*Let us then fearlessly and confidently and boldly draw near to the throne of grace—the throne of*

God's unmerited favor [to us sinners]; that we may receive mercy [for our failures] and find grace to help in good time for every need—appropriate help and well-timed help, coming just when we need it."

The story is told of a child born with a tear duct that was too small so that the fluid from her right eye did not drain properly. Her grandparents laid hands on her and prayed over it but saw no visible results for almost two years. One day, while studying the blood covenant, one of the grandparents reminded the Lord of the situation in prayer and then declared aloud for the enemy Satan to hear, "This child is part of our family and is in the blood covenant. This tear duct has to yield to the power of the blood. This has gone on long enough! Satan, get your hands off this situation, the blood of Jesus is against you and is applied, by faith, to this eye duct." On the next visit to the doctor, the eye was completely clear of drainage which had collected in her eye on a regular basis.

Believer as Priest Proclaiming the Blood Covenant

Scripture makes it clear the believer is a priest. 1 Peter 2:5 AMP states, "*[Come] and as living stones be yourselves built into a spiritual house for a holy (dedicated, consecrated) priesthood, to offer up [those] spiritual sacrifices [that are] acceptable and well pleasing to God through Jesus Christ.*" We are also ministers of reconciliation according to 2 Corinthians 5:18 NIV. It tells us we are reconciled (brought into harmony) to God though Jesus Christ and we have a ministry of reconciliation—that by word and deed we might aspire to bring others into harmony with Him. "*All this is from God, who reconciled us to himself through Christ and gave us the ministry of reconciliation.*" We place our trust in the finished work of the cross and we proclaim that message of reconciliation out to the world in our daily walk with the Lord.

We must call on the blood of Jesus where there is stress or any action that opposes God's will on earth. "*You have come to Jesus, the one who mediates the new covenant between God and people, and to the sprinkled blood, which graciously forgives instead of crying out for vengeance as the blood of Abel did*" (Hebrews 12:24 NLT).

Satan is behind all damage to our bodies whether directly or indirectly. He tempts us with bad health habits, passivity to exercise, proneness to worry, and anxiety. W.H. Whyte teaches that when the blood of Jesus is applied in faith, it acts as a covering and "the natural healing processes in our body quickly do their work, for they are not hindered by Satan. The blood of Jesus is the finest covering and disinfectant in the world. It is perfect!"[1]

Whyte also states that: "When the blood covers us and we know it and we have placed it by faith upon our hearts, lives, homes, and loved ones, then we have created a condition where Satan cannot get through. So keep under the blood! This is one substance all the devils in hell cannot penetrate. But it is not automatically obtained—we must claim it by faith and maintain it by continuing in that faith. We are not to let down our faith in the blood. There is more power in the blood than anyone ever imagined."[2]

Whyte's strongest Scriptural reference is Zechariah 13:1, which speaks of a fountain that "is described as a river, a continually flowing river into which we may plunge daily to wash away our sins and sicknesses and sorrows. This stream ever flows before Satan and all his host; and as we honor it, sing about it, talk about it, plead it out loud, the blood of Jesus pleads mercy, forgiveness, pardon, healing, protection, deliverance and multiplied joy and peace." [3]

We believe in the historic blood of Calvary and we also believe the power made available by that fountain of the precious blood of Jesus is available today by faith. We avail ourselves of its power and life by faith. We proclaim it to enforce Jesus' victory over Satan in every aspect of our lives. The havoc in the life of a child of God is addressed through a personal declaration of the power of the blood covenant. During the Old Testament Passover, the blood applied to the doorpost provided the means for peace of mind. It took away the power of the destroyer. It was the applied blood that halted the destroyer. Action was required in putting the blood on the doorposts of the dwellings.

So it is with the blood of the Lord Jesus Christ. It is effective in the life of the believer on a day-to-day basis when the person declares his faith in the victory over Satan secured at the cross by Jesus. Colossians 2:15 NKJV—"*Having disarmed principalities and powers, He made a public spectacle of them, triumphing over them in it.*" Revelation 12:11 NIV states, "*They overcame him by the blood of the Lamb and by the word of their testimony; and they did not love their lives so much as to shrink from death.*"

Three guidelines are presented in this Scripture. 1) The basis of our power and authority over the enemy is the blood of the Lamb. 2) The word of our testimony is the *speaking aloud* of scripture to our adversary declaring what the blood of Jesus provided for us as His followers. Jesus demonstrated this pattern for us in the wilderness when He used the sword of the Spirit (the word) against Satan. He said, "*It is written*" as He responded to the temptations. (Matthew 4:3) We deal with the "self life" when we declare we love not our own lives.

Under the protection of the blood of the Lord Jesus Christ, and through the authority He imparted to us, we notify Satan he is a defeated foe. God promised His people that He will deliver them from the destroyer when He sees the blood (the Passover account discussed previously in chapter six). God keeps His promises. Our responsibility and privilege is to declare the victory over Satan that Jesus' death on the cross secured. "*Submit yourselves, then to God. Resist the devil, and he will flee from you*" (James 4:7 NIV).

While washing her hair under the kitchen sink, my friend, Brenda turned her head in such a way that water went into her left ear very forcefully causing *complete* loss of hearing. The doctor treated her with medication but her hearing did not return. She then went to an ear specialist who told her "You are deaf in this ear! This just happens sometimes for no reason. There is nothing that will help. You will just have to get used to it."

Brenda immediately thought of the men Moses sent out to spy the land of Canaan. (Numbers 13). Caleb said, "*We are well able to overcome . . .*" but the men who went up with him brought an evil report. Brenda decided she would not receive a bad report regardless of its medical basis. *She did not let the words* of the doctor *take "root"* in her. Psalms 112:7,8 NIV says of the man who fears the Lord: "*He will have no fear of bad news; his heart is steadfast trusting in the*

Lord. His heart is secure, he will have no fear; in the end he will look in triumph on his foes."

Brenda asked others to stand with her in prayer including an elder who anointed her with oil and prayed for complete restoration of her hearing. He reported the prayer for healing just seemed to gush out of him. Brenda felt movement in her ear as he prayed.

Following this prayer, Brenda began to attack the enemy who tries to kill, steal, and destroy. (John 10:10) The Lord uses Brenda in a ministry of listening to hurting, troubled, anxious people, especially by telephone. Satan would have loved to thwart that ministry. Like a good soldier, she went to battle enforcing the law of redemption which she believes includes provision for her body as well as for her spirit. She picked up the sword of the spirit (Ephesians 6) and attacked Satan with it.

Three times a day Brenda anointed her ear with oil and declared the power of the blood over this affliction. She recounts standing and looking at herself in the mirror and literally *preaching the healing word of Scripture to her ear.* "This ear is whole in the name of Jesus. It has perfect hearing because Jesus died to provide for my physical as well as for my spiritual wholeness. I will not allow Satan to come and steal, kill, and destroy my hearing. I am a child of the most High God—El-Elyon. The precious blood of Jesus bought me. As God's daughter, I have every right to expect this ear to hear. This left ear problem will bow to the name of Jesus and His will. His will is for me to hear."

The Lord had led Brenda to Matthew 11:5 which declares that *"the deaf hear,"* Brenda declared this promise a number of times over her ear with the belief that Jesus had pain in His ears on the cross to cover this affliction. Blood ran down and covered His ears. "He deposited all I need on the day he died. It is in my account. I have to draw on it. I am healed by the stripes of Jesus (Isaiah 53). I know I have my hearing. I see myself with perfect hearing."

During this time Brenda's husband came home from an overseas job. She asked him to lay hands on her ear and pray over it, which he willingly did. Their daughter was getting married during this time, and it would have been easy for Brenda to think she was too busy to focus on this hearing problem. This did not happen. She went after this healing with the Word of the Lord, knowing the Word will not return void (Isaiah 55:11). After four weeks, her hearing was completely restored as it became progressively better over the last few days of this period. She was using the Word as medicine (Proverbs 4:20). Medicine does not always take care of the symptoms immediately as it is working on the disease at the source.

Brenda says that she now has an enlarged compassion for people with negative reports. She has been empowered with more of a heart for hurting people. She has walked through training that God will use as she ministers to others.

The fountain of blood was provided at Calvary but it must be *activated by confession*. (We have understood the importance of confession for receiving Jesus as Savior.) Now we come to understand receiving Jesus as healer. Just as you have water in a water fountain (in a country with adequate water supply), you have to turn the handle to start the water bubbling up. We, too, as believers, draw on the fountain of blood provided by Jesus Christ's sacrificial death on the cross. The fountain starts to flow in the spirit realm as we *audibly declare our faith in the power of the blood.*

Whyte believes that "If every Christian who names the name of Jesus would plead His precious blood every day *out loud,* the result would be catastrophic in Satan's Kingdom and great deliverance would be felt in the church and the nation."[4] This also extends to our private lives as well. We remind ourselves to stay under the blood protection through faith and obedience. Our Father will hear His children when we stand on earth and sound the blood cry. Our enemy is turned back when we proclaim the blood sacrifice of our Lord and Savior Jesus Christ.

I am indebted to the renowned Bible scholar, Derek Prince for the following.

Confession for Overcomers

My body is a temple for the Holy Spirit, redeemed, cleansed, and sanctified by the Blood of Jesus. My members, the parts of my body, are instruments of righteousness, yielded to God for His service and for His glory. The devil has no place in me, no power over me, no unsettled claims against me. All has been settled by the Blood of Jesus. I overcome Satan by the Blood of the lamb, and by the word of my testimony, and I love not my life unto the death. My body is for the Lord and the Lord is for my body. Amen.

As you will recognize, all these statements are the pure Word of God from various Scriptures.

I have had two dramatic experiences of victory using this confession of the Word.

My husband, daughter, and I were traveling and stopped for overnight. I awakened about 4 A.M. racked with severe pain in my left mid-back area. The pain was unmistakably related to a kidney stone, which I had experienced before. As I thrashed around in the bed, trying to get into a position which would offer some relief, my husband awakened. I asked him to lay hands on me and pray for me.

I am a nurse by profession and believe in practical measures as well as the spiritual. I got in the shower and let the hottest water I could stand beat down on the pained area. For 15–20 minutes I proclaimed the Overcomer's Confession, which I had committed to memory.

I said this audibly while the hot water ran on my back. I was combining a scriptural declaration with a practical comfort measure. After about fifteen minutes of speaking the Word, the pain was completely gone and has never recurred in the ensuing 12–15 years.

The second experience with this powerful declaration of Scriptures occurred at a Celebrate Jesus board meeting, where I served in the capacity of prayer chairman. As prayer requests were given, the leader assigned me to pray for a gentleman who held up his hand and said he was in severe pain from a kidney stone. I sat trying to discern how to pray—being one of only two lay women in the room in the midst of a number of pastors of various denominations. I was a little intimidated and didn't feel I could rise up in a full gospel, "shake-the-rafters" kind of prayer. When it was my time to pray, I tapped the shoulder of one of the ministers so he would join me.

Another man came as we circled the table where Gary sat. The two of them laid hands on Gary, anointed him with oil and prayed. Then I said, "I need to stop for a moment and share my kidney stone experience" which I did very briefly. Then I said, "I want to proclaim the Overcomer's Confession over Gary, which I did inserting his name where appropriate.

The Lord had prompted me to take one of the printed Overcomer's Confession cards to the meeting that day. I left it with Gary after the proclamation. About twenty minutes further into the meeting, Gary raised his hand and said, "I have a praise report: the pain is gone." I see Gary frequently and he testifies the pain has never returned in the two-plus intervening years. It is good to remind ourselves that the Word of God is our sword (Ephesians 6:17). I was speaking the pure Word of God over Gary, not my own thoughts. *"God sent His Word and healed them"* (Psalms 107:20). We were within scriptural guidelines as the pastor and elder laid hands on him and anointed him with oil. There were a number of scriptural principles present here including proclamation of the power of the blood.

Would You Be Free

Would you be free from the burden of sin?
There's power in the blood, pow'r in the blood;
Would you o'er evil a victory win?
There's wonderful pow'r in the blood.
Would you be free from your passion and pride?
There's pow'r in the blood, pow'r in the blood;
Come for a cleansing to Calvary's tide
There's wonderful pow'r in the blood.

Would you be whiter, much whiter than snow
There's pow'r in the blood, pow'r in the blood;
Sin stains are lost in its life giving flow,
There's wonderful pow'r in the blood.
Would you do service for Jesus your King?
There's pow'r in the blood, pow'r in the blood,
Would you live daily His praises to sing?
There's wonderful pow'r in the blood.

Chorus

There is power, pow'r, wonder working pow'r
In the blood of the Lamb;
There is pow'r, pow'r, wonder working pow'r
In the precious blood of the Lamb.

L.E. Jones
Great Songs of the Church—Number Two
Standard Publishing

One night in a church service a young woman felt the tug of God at her heart. She responded to God's call and accepted Jesus as her Lord and Savior. The young woman had a very rough past, involving alcohol, drugs, and prostitution. But the change in her was evident. As time went on she became a faithful member of the church. She eventually became involved in the ministry teaching young children. It was not very long until this faithful young woman had caught the eye and heart of the pastor's son. Their relationship grew and they began to make wedding plans.

However, problems began as about one half of the church did not think that a woman with a past such as hers was suitable as a wife for the pastor's son. The church began to argue and fight about the matter, which lead to a meeting. The meeting got completely out of hand with tension building during the arguments. The young woman became very upset over all the things being brought up about her past. She began to cry. The young man could not stand to see his beloved in such pain. He stated, "My fiancee's past is not what is on trial here. What you are questioning is the ability of the blood of Jesus to wash away sin. Today you have put the blood of Jesus on trial. So, does it wash away sin or not?" The whole church began to weep as they realized they had been slandering the blood of the Lord Jesus Christ.

Too often, even as Christians, we bring up the past and use it as a weapon against our brothers and sisters. Forgiveness is a very foundational part of the gospel of our Lord Jesus Christ. If the blood of Jesus does not cleanse the person in question completely, then it cannot cleanse us completely. If that is the case, then we are all in serious trouble. What can wash away my sins? Nothing but the blood of Jesus. There is no case or charge that can be brought against the *blood-bought* child of God!

Celebrating the Victory Through Communion

Jesus and His disciples were celebrating Passover together in the upper room. The time was at hand when Jesus, the Lamb of God (John 1:36) would offer His blood as a sacrifice for the sins of all mankind (Mark 14:16–26, Matthew 26:17–30). We remember it was at the Passover, as the Israelites prepared to leave Egypt (Exodus 12), they ate of a sacrificial lamb without spot or blemish.. The father was commanded to apply the blood of the lamb to their doorposts so that God's judgment would pass over their homes. Communion pictures this Passover act: we partake of the bread representing Jesus' body and drink the fruit of the vine representing His blood.

It was at this time that Jesus instituted what is known in the Protestant churches as the Lord's Supper or Communion, known in the Catholic Church as the Holy Eucharist. He took bread, gave thanks, broke it and said, "'This is my body which is for you; do this in remembrance of me.' In the same way, after supper he took the cup, saying, 'This cup is the covenant in my blood; do this, whenever you drink it, in remembrance of me.' For whenever you eat this bread and drink this cup, you proclaim the Lord's death until he comes'" (1 Corinthians 11:24–26 NIV). As believers in Christ we have the wonderful promise in Jesus' words in John 6:54–56 NIV, "I tell you the truth, unless you eat the flesh of the Son of Man and drink his blood, you have no life in you. Whoever eats my flesh and drinks my blood has eternal life, and I will raise him up at the last day. For my flesh is real food and my blood is real drink. Whoever eats my flesh and drinks my blood remains in me, and I in him."

Remembering

Each time we come to the Lord's table, it is an occasion for confession of faith in Jesus' sacrifice. We are calling to remembrance the Lord's death—proclaiming the benefits of Jesus' redemption over our lives. We have the opportunity to call to memory and appropriate the benefits Jesus' death provided for us and for all those who receive Him as Lord and Savior.

God desires that communion be a time of intimacy with Christ. We enter into His presence with awe in great reverence and thankfulness with our hearts focused on Christ and His ministry of total salvation. We have the privilege of entering into a supernatural union with Jesus as we receive the bread and cup. It is a sacred meeting with Christ where we experience a bond of fellowship. We enter the divine presence with our hearts focused upon Christ and His ministry of salvation. It is a "supper of memory." When we look at the bread and cup we travel back in time to the cross and the memory of the Passover time when the perfect Lamb was sacrificed. He was the lamb slain from the foundation of the world. (Revelation 13:8) We kneel in our spirit at the foot of the cross, and by faith the healing rays come off the cross and cover us as we wrap the righteousness of Jesus around us. We bask in His presence.

Self Examination/Discerning the Lord's Body

We are cautioned to examine ourselves so as not to eat and drink in an unworthy manner. We examine our life asking God to reveal to us any sins that need to be confessed, repented of, and renounced (1 John 1:9). Communion offers us a spiritual cleansing.

We bring judgment upon ourselves if we do not discern the Lord's body. We are cautioned in 1 Corinthians 11:29 that we open ourselves up to weakness, sickness, and death (premature) if we do not discern the body of Jesus. Isaiah 53:5b AMP clearly states: "*With the stripes that wounded Him, we are healed and made whole.*" His body was bruised, beaten, and pierced for our sickness/physical affliction.

Physical wholeness is part of the redemptive work of Christ. Matthew 8:17 and again 1 Peter 2:24 make it clear that Jesus bore our diseases. He sustained in His body wounds to provide for my physical well being, and out of those wounds His blood flowed to cover my sins.

We also recognize that we are part of the body of Christ—believers all over the world who are also in the blood covenant. We acknowledge our spiritual union within that body who are also partakers of Jesus' body and blood. Remember that Christ is the head of the church and we are members dependent on Him and on one another. We are part of His body and are to dwell in unity in the family of God. The Holy Spirit makes unity possible. It is the responsibility of each believer to do his or her part to maintain the unity.

Partaking

When we partake of the cup we celebrate His taking our sins. When we partake of the bread, we draw on the healing listed in Psalm 103:3 as the second benefit of the Lord. We exchange weakness for strength, inadequacy for adequacy. The divine exchange is there, but we must recognize it and draw on it. We are, by faith, feeding on the life of Jesus as we take the bread and cup into our own bodies. We are drawing on His life.

Indeed He is our life. We, by faith, draw on the healing rays that come off the cross.

The Cross of Calvary

By your stripes I have been healed
By the blood that flowed down from your head
By your wounded side and nail-scarred hands
To reveal to me redemption's plan
I begin to see your heart towards man
How you died for me so I could stand in you.

The cross of Calvary it stands for victory
It stands eternally for all to see
The cross of Calvary has made a way for me
And sets this captive free to honor thee.

Words and music by Matthew Ward and Ann Herring
Copyright 2002 Megin's College Fund Music and Latter
Day Rain
Journey of My Heart Album / Kelly Wilkerson Vocalist

When we celebrate communion, we recall the benefits provided by His sacrifice on Calvary. We proclaim the power of the cross in our lives, as well as proclaim Jesus' triumph over Satan at the cross. We take refuge in the shadow of the cross. We enter the divine presence with our heart focused upon Christ and His ministry of salvation. We are committed to share that life wherever he provides opportunity. Jesus' blood is a mighty spiritual force that binds the believer to God in blood covenant.

PRAYER Father, help us to stand up in the victory that radiates from the cross as it casts a shadow in which we may take refuge.

References

1. Maxwell Whyte, *The Power of the Blood*, New Kensington, PA, Whitaker House, 1973, p. 53
2. Ibid p. 52
3. Ibid p. 58
4. Ibid p. 61

Resources Consulted

Alsobrook, David, *The Precious Blood*, Sure Word Ministries, Brentwood, Tennessee Revised Edition 1993

Bagwell, Dr. Tim, *When I See The Blood*, McDougal Publishing, Hagerstown, MD, 1998

Coleman, Dr. Robert E., *The New Covenant*, Christian Outreach, Deerfield, IL, 1984

Hagin, Kenneth, *The Precious Blood of Jesus*, (pamphlet), Kenneth Hagin Ministries, Tulsa, OK. 1992

Hickey, Marilyn, *The Power of the Blood; A Physician's Analysis*, Marilyn Hickey Ministries, 1987

Hinn, Benny, *The Blood*, Creation House, Orlando, FL, 1993

Hinn, Benny, Tapes Series *The Blood, How to Remove Plagues, Applying The Blood, Results of the Blood,* Benny Hinn Ministries, Orlando, FL

Kenyon, E.W., *The Blood Covenant,* Kenyon's Gospel Publishing Society, Lynnwood, WA, 1997

Meyer, Joyce, *The Word, The Name, The Blood,* Harrison House, Tulsa, OK, 1995

Murray, Andrew, *The Power of the Blood of Jesus,* Whitaker House, Springdale, PA, 1993

Shaw, Gwen, *The Power of the Precious Blood,* End Time Handmaidens, Inc., Jasper, AK, 1978

Spurgeon, Charles, *Power in the Blood,* Whitaker House, New Kensington, PA, 1996

Whyte, H.A. Maxwell, *The Power of the Blood,* Whitaker House, New Kensington, PA, 1973

The author wanted her study to reflect a broad range of streams of Christian thought to be prayerfully considered as she did the writing. This does not indicate a recommendation of everything read but to let the reader know she did read extensively **after** studying all scripture relating to the blood.

Additional Testimonies

*J*ackie and her husband went to France to spend vacation time with their daughter who was living there. They rented a heavy BMW car and went out into the countryside. Jackie's husband is very adventuresome and decided to take a short cut which led down a road that became smaller and smaller. As they went further, the road turned into a gravel driveway with a no trespassing sign. There were no cars or houses for miles. James decided to turn around and in doing so one of the wheels sled into a culvert with a deep ravine on one side. The chassis of the car was resting on metal and the ravine was threatening them. If the car were moved very much, they would go over the side of the culvert into the creek below. Jackie had recently read Kay Arthur's book on covenant. She started to pray, remembering that she is in blood covenant with God. Part of the covenant is, "What is yours is mine." In the primitive ceremony, coats and weapons were exchanged and the covenanting parties took the name of the other as a middle name to further identify with each other. Jackie remembered her covenant benefits and said, "I am weak, You are strong. We are asking for Your plan. We don't know what to do. You are our faith, You are our provision. We know You have a plan and we call on You and Your wisdom. We call on everything You have to get us out of this situation." Suddenly a car appeared with two young boys and one girl who offered to help. Jackie's daughter moved into the driver's seat of the stick shift car. James and the two boys positioned themselves to lift up on the bumper in back. Jackie continued to call on her covenant God for His perfect provision and to thank Him. The heavy car came right up off the culvert as they lifted and the daughter drove forward. Jackie stated in recounting this, "We knew our covenant partner was taking care of us no matter what."

Sara gave me the following testimony; I claim the blood of Jesus so frequently that I can't remember exact times. I do know that I claim it most when I am afraid, frightened, feeling agitated, lonely, sad, or feel the presence of evil. It always brings me peace and well-being. When I was going through a very ugly and long divorce, I was so weary I would picture myself at the foot of the cross and the blood of Jesus covering me. (I am one who gets weak when I see blood, so it's amazing how this helps me.) I even claim the blood in my dreams when I'm afraid, frightened, or need protection from evil. Whenever I feel the possible presence of evil in my dreams or in real life experiences, I immediately claim the blood protection. I am always at peace and assured after I do this.

One night while going through my divorce, I was staying in the home of a friend while she was out of town for the summer. Just before this incident happened, I was awakened and started praising the Lord for about 15–30 minutes. Later in the night I had a vision that my "husband" was possessed and was levitating my prayer journal pages on the twin bed next to me. He started coming to me in a semi-circle and I sat up in bed claiming the blood of Jesus pointing at him the entire time. The vision kept coming toward me, but got smaller and smaller and disappeared when it got right beside me. The thought came that it was going to spring up again in full figure before me, but it didn't. I was completely at peace and went back to sleep until morning.

Edna related to me that her eight-year-old daughter had to be taken from Indonesia to Thailand to see a specialist for a severe bowel problem. Edna's husband couldn't leave his job, so Edna had to go alone. She was there through two surgeries extending over five weeks. When her daughter was discharged, Edna had to travel by plane back to Indonesia. She was told her child's stomach could "pop open" from the pressure in the plane. Her daughter's stomach did start to swell in flight. Edna started proclaiming the protecting power of the blood of Jesus over the situation and calling on her covenant God for help. They arrived without any problem with the incision.

Jane told me of a situation her pastor son faced. A very disturbed and troubled young woman in her twenties, whom he had never met, starting calling him. Dan had been told she was mentally ill. She called often and he would minister to her by phone. Eventually she requested that he come to visit her at her parent's home.

Dan very wisely asked his mother to accompany him. On the way over they discussed how they would minister the love of God and how they would speak of the blood of Jesus which they believed would quiet any evil spirits responsible for her erratic behavior.

The young woman met them at the door obviously disturbed that Jane had come along. She was jumpy and shaky, acting in a very erratic manner. At times she was very loud, sometimes she would sob. She could not sit still, kept moving from one chair to another, and at one time sat on the floor. This behavior went on for the first ten to fifteen minutes while they tried to tell her about the love of God and how Jesus could set her free from the turmoil she was in. She seemed so disconnected they knew their words were falling on deaf ears.

Then Jane and Dan started to talk about the blood of Jesus in every sentence. Sometimes they were just saying "The Blood of Jesus" and nothing else to her. It was when they began this intensity of speaking of the blood, that they saw calmness come over her in a way that was indescribable. Her whole body became relaxed. Her countenance changed. She stopped shaking. She stopped moving around. She stopped uttering statements that made no sense. She became a true listener and seemed to "connect" to what was being said and to ask questions over the next two hours of ministry to her.

Jane never knew the outcome of the story since the young woman attended another church with her parents.

She called Dan a time or two more. He did not initiate calls to her because she was obviously infatuated with him.

Jane said, "There is no way to describe the change that came over her as we spoke of the blood of Jesus repeatedly."

Liz was on a plane recently when a bad storm arose. Whenever she flies she starts the journey by saying, "In the name of Jesus I proclaim the blood and the lordship of Jesus over this plane." She also asks for angels to minister to the mechanics and the pilots. In addition she declares that she is an ambassador for Christ to minister to those He brings across her path.

On this particular flight, the plane was in a holding pattern for landing, a storm was raging, and the landing gear and flaps would not come down. The plane had twenty minutes of fuel left. Liz started declaring that she is a blood covenant woman and has a covenant of peace according to Isaiah 54:10. She started quoting Psalms 91 which is the believer's 911 for emergencies. All around her was a sea of anxiety and confusion. Fear was rampant.

Two landings were attempted and aborted because of wind shear. The pilot was directed to another airport nearby where fire engines were waiting. Again the landing gear and flaps would not come down. The fuel was dwindling. The pilot announced he would have to take the plane in fast so the force on impact would slow it down. Liz continued to make proclamations over herself and the situation. The plane landed without incident and the shaken passengers quickly disembarked. Liz was praising her covenant God.

Liz related another experience. She was in an unfamiliar subway station in Washington, D.C. Due to an unusual set of circumstances, she had a very heavy tote bag containing dinner for her daughter's family. She was on the train ready to depart, seated next to a young woman. Liz described her as being greasy and unkempt looking, dressed in baggy blue pants with new-age symbols and new-age-looking jewelry. Suddenly the announcement came to vacate the train and the terminal immediately. The two went together up a long flight of steps, the heavy bag in tow. Liz started to claim the power of the blood over the situation. The announcement rang out, "The terminal is closed, there has been an accident, there will be no more cars coming, everyone must leave immediately, vacate now."

Pandemonium broke out. There was a myriad of emotions, people screaming, yelling, and trying to jump over the turnstile. Suddenly the young woman grabbed Liz's arm saying, "A subway is coming." Liz had heard nothing but she ran hurriedly down the long flight of stairs. Miraculously, out of nowhere, a train appeared. Liz and the girl boarded and arrived safely at their destination with no further incident. God had heard and answered Liz's prayer for protection in the midst of this confusion.

Many of us have an ATM bank card to withdraw money deposited in our account; likewise we may, by faith, draw on the deposit of benefits laid up for us by the blood of our Savior, the Lord Jesus Christ. The prayer card below was designed so you can cut it out, laminate it and carry it with you as a reminder to call on the blood covenant in your daily life.

Suggested Daily Prayer

Father, I come to you in the name of the ♦ Lord ♦ Jesus Christ ♦ I thank you for the mighty provision of the blood shed for all mankind at the cross. Through the power of the Holy Spirit living within me, by faith, I claim the blood of Jesus over my life, ♦ my family, and ♦ over all of which you have made me steward. ♦ I declare that the redeeming blood of Jesus covers ♦ my mind, body, emotions, will, ♦ relationships, and finances and that the blood is a covering between me and any schemes of the evil one. Amen

Dear Reader,

God has you in mind when He moved on my heart to write this book on *The Power of the Lamb's Blood*. His love reaches out to you at this moment. He longs to be your heavenly Father. If you have never accepted Jesus Christ as your Lord and Savior would you pray with me now the prayer of salvation?

Prayer for Salvation

Dear God, I recognize and confess I have sinned. I ask You to forgive every sin I have ever committed. I thank You that you provided the blood sacrifice for my sins through the death of Your son, Jesus Christ, the Lamb of God. By faith I receive Your wonderful provision to save me from eternal damnation. I also believe it saves me to experience eternal life with You. I invite Jesus to come into my life and be my Lord and Savior. I thank You that according to John 1:12 I have the right to become Your child because I believe in and confess Your name. I will follow Jesus' example and enter the waters of baptism and come up a new creation—born again—a son/daughter of God.

Standing Strong in Your Decision

1. Read the Bible daily – praying for insight and understanding (Acts 17:11).
2. Pray about everything (Philippians 4:6-7).
3. Unite with a God-honoring body of believers where the Bible is accepted and preached as the infallible Word of God (Hebrews 10:25).
4. Cultivate a lifestyle of praise and worship (Psalms 107:1,2).
5. Be a doer of the Word and not a hearer only (James 1:22).
6. Witness – go forth and live out your confession of Jesus Christ as Lord and Savior through the power of the Holy Spirit who dwells in each believer—testifying to His saving grace wherever the opportunity presents itself (Mark 16:15).

To order additional copies of

Park Praise Publications
PO Box 22101
Lexington, KY 40522

parkpraisepublications@insightbb.com or
www.parkpraisepublications.com

$14.99 plus $2.99 S&H
6% sales tax in Kentucky

Available by special order through any book store